ANIMALS AT RISK!

Snow Leopards

by Rachel Grack

BELLWETHER MEDIA • MINNEAPOLIS, MN

BLASTOFF!
2
READERS

Blastoff! Readers are carefully developed by literacy experts to build reading stamina and move students toward fluency by combining standards-based content with developmentally appropriate text.

Level 1 provides the most support through repetition of high-frequency words, light text, predictable sentence patterns, and strong visual support.

Level 2 offers early readers a bit more challenge through varied sentences, increased text load, and text-supportive special features.

Level 3 advances early-fluent readers toward fluency through increased text load, less reliance on photos, advancing concepts, longer sentences, and more complex special features.

★ **Blastoff! Universe**

Reading Level

Grade **K**

Grades **1–3**

Grade **4**

This edition first published in 2023 by Bellwether Media, Inc.

No part of this publication may be reproduced in whole or in part without written permission of the publisher. For information regarding permission, write to Bellwether Media, Inc., Attention: Permissions Department, 6012 Blue Circle Drive, Minnetonka, MN 55343.

Library of Congress Cataloging-in-Publication Data

Names: Koestler-Grack, Rachel A., 1973- author.
Title: Snow leopards / by Rachel Grack.
Description: Minneapolis, MN : Bellwether Media, Inc., 2023. | Series: Blastoff! Readers. Animals at risk | Includes bibliographical references and index. | Audience: Ages 5-8 | Audience: Grades 2-3 | Summary: "Relevant images match informative text in this introduction to snow leopards. Intended for students in kindergarten through third grade"-- Provided by publisher.
Identifiers: LCCN 2022037563 (print) | LCCN 2022037564 (ebook) | ISBN 9798886871203 (library binding) | ISBN 9798886872460 (ebook)
Subjects: LCSH: Snow leopard--Conservation--Juvenile literature.
Classification: LCC QL737.C23 K644 2023 (print) | LCC QL737.C23 (ebook) | DDC 599.75/55--dc23/eng/20220809
LC record available at https://lccn.loc.gov/2022037563
LC ebook record available at https://lccn.loc.gov/2022037564

Editor: Kieran Downs   Designer: Brittany McIntosh

Printed in the United States of America, North Mankato, MN.

Table of Contents

Disappearing Cats

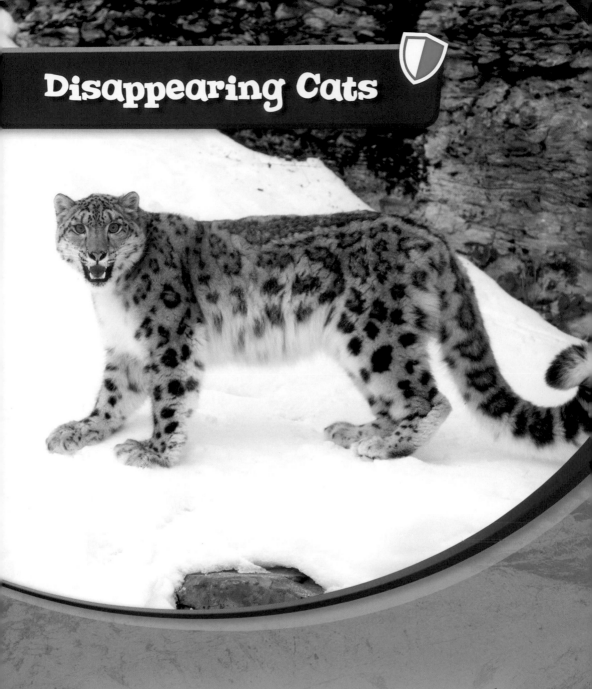

Snow leopards are big cats with spotted fur. They live in the snowy mountains of Central Asia.

Their grayish **coats** blend into their **habitat**. They seem to disappear against the snow!

Many snow leopards once lived in the wild. Today, they are a **vulnerable species**.

People have caused
most of their troubles.

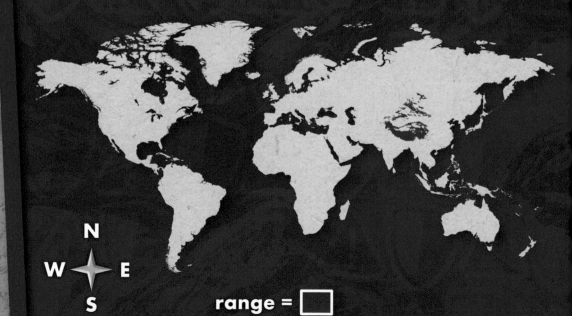

Snow Leopard
Range

N
W
E
S

range = ☐

livestock

Snow leopards need large **home ranges**. But people use their habitat for **livestock** and mining.

8

Climate change also destroys snow leopard habitats.

 Threats

people need land for livestock

snow leopards hunt livestock

farmers hunt snow leopards

Poachers kill snow leopards for their beautiful fur. Some people use snow leopard bones in **traditional** medicines.

Farmers also harm snow leopards to keep their livestock safe.

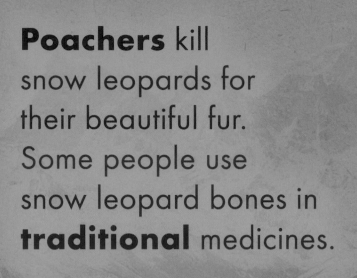

snow leopard fur

10

Snow Leopard Stats

Least Concern	Near Threatened	Vulnerable	Endangered	Critically Endangered	Extinct in the Wild	Extinct

conservation status: vulnerable

life span: around 10 years

Save the Snow Leopards!

Snow leopards keep mountain **ecosystems** healthy. They hunt wild sheep and goats.

Without them, sheep and goats would eat too many plants. Other animals would have less food.

The World with Snow Leopards

1 more snow leopards

2 healthy number of wild sheep and goats

3 healthy number of plants

Governments set aside **reserves** for snow leopards. These lands give snow leopards plenty of space and food.

People cannot farm or mine on reserves. **Rangers** keep poachers away.

Wildlife workers teach farmers
safe ways to raise animals.

They show farmers fenced pens.
These keep snow leopards out.
Livestock and snow leopards
stay safe!

fenced pen

New **laws** also help snow leopards. People must respect snow leopards' mountain homes.

It is illegal to buy snow leopard furs. The number of snow leopards is slowly growing!

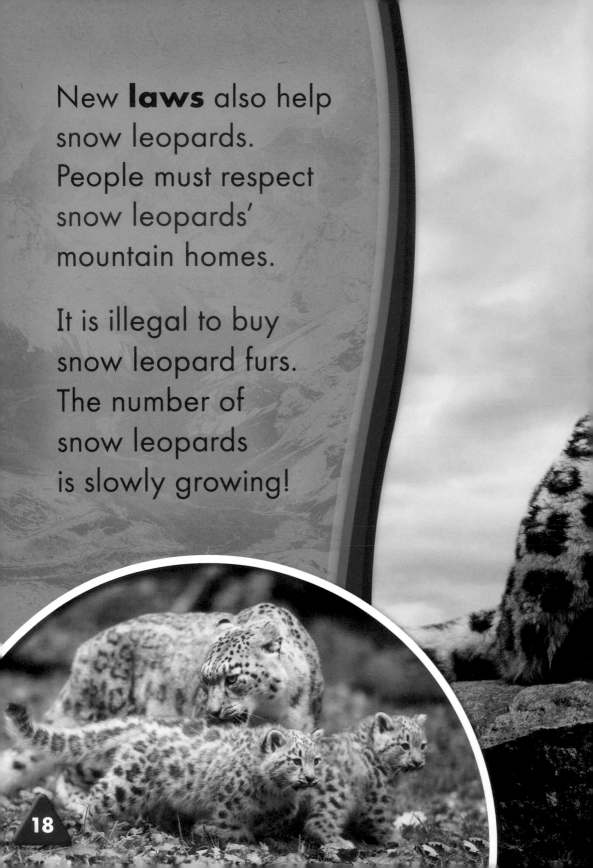

Everyone can help save snow leopards. Wildlife groups count on **donations**.

Using less **energy** slows climate change. With help, these **apex predators** will not disappear!

Glossary

apex predators—animals at the top of the food chain that are not preyed upon by other animals

climate change—a human-caused changed in Earth's weather due to warming temperatures

coats—the hair or fur covering some animals

donations—gifts, usually money

ecosystems—communities of plants and animals living in certain places

energy—the power to make things work

habitat—the place where animals live

home ranges—the lands on which a group of animals lives and travels

laws—rules that must be followed

livestock—animals kept on a farm

poachers—people who hunt illegally

rangers—people in charge of protecting an area of land

reserves—areas of land set aside for wild animals

traditional—related to customs, ideas, or beliefs passed down from one generation to the next

vulnerable species—animals at risk of becoming endangered

To Learn More

AT THE LIBRARY

Bodden, Valerie. *Snow Leopards*. Mankato, Minn.: Creative Education, 2022.

Geister-Jones, Sophie. *Snow Leopards*. Mendota Heights, Minn.: Apex, 2021.

Shaffer, Lindsay. *Snow Leopards*. Minneapolis, Minn.: Bellwether Media, 2020.

ON THE WEB

FACTSURFER

Factsurfer.com gives you a safe, fun way to find more information.

1. Go to www.factsurfer.com.

2. Enter "snow leopards" into the search box and click 🔍.

3. Select your book cover to see a list of related content.

Index

The images in this book are reproduced through the courtesy of: Eric Isselee, front cover, p. 3; Jim Cumming, p. 4; Dennis W Donohue, p. 5; Arterra Picture Library/ Alamy Stock Photo, p. 6; Yunqing Shi, p. 8; beibaoke, p. 9 (top left); Thorsten Spoerlein, p. 9 (top right); Michal Lukaszewicz, p. 9 (bottom); TheWonderWays, p. 10; Warren Metcalf, pp. 10-11; Rudy Mateeuwsen/ Getty Images, p. 12; Steve Bloom Images/ Alamy Stock Photo, p. 13 (top left); Anton Jankovoy, p. 13 (top right); Daniel J. Rao, p. 13 (bottom); Vince Burton/ Alamy Stock Photo, p. 14; Jack Bell Photography, p. 15; CPRESS PHOTO LIMITED/ Alamy Stock Photo, p. 16; Nick Garbutt/ Nature Picture Library, p. 17; blickwinkel/ Alamy Stock Photo, p. 18; Ondrej Prosicky, pp. 18-19; Imagebroker/ Alamy Stock Photo, p. 20; Gerard Lacz/ VWPics/ Alamy Stock Photo, p. 21; clarst5, p. 23.